Edwina was born in Portsmouth into a naval family. When she was four, the family moved to Nottingham, her father being posted there as Royal Navy and Royal Marine Recruiting Officer. In the time before eleven plus exams, she took a scholarship and won a place at Brincliffe Grammar School in Nottingham. On marriage, she moved to Derbyshire with her husband Geoffrey, who was a draughtsman at Rolls-Royce (Aero Division) Ltd. After their two sons were settled at school Edwina also joined the staff at Rolls-Royce. In the early seventies, the family moved to Cornwall where she still lives and enjoys village life but sadly is now widowed.

Dedication

For James's grandchildren

Michael Gascoigne, Anne Davis, Lynne Gascoigne,

James (Jim) Pogson and Garry Pogson

With memories of their late parents May Gascoigne and
Geoffrey Pogson

Edwina Pogson

FLOWERS FOR THE DUCHESS

AUSTIN MACAULEY PUBLISHERS™

LONDON • CAMBRIDGE • NEW YORK • SHARJAH

A CIP catalogue record for this title is available from the British
Library.

ISBN 9781788481618 (Paperback)
ISBN 9781788481625 (Hardback)
ISBN 9781788481632 (E-Book)

www.austinmacauley.com

First Published (2018)
Austin Macauley Publishers Ltd™
25 Canada Square
Canary Wharf
London
E14 5LQ

Acknowledgements

My thanks to my husband's nieces, Anne Davis and Lynne Gascoigne, for kindly passing James's diary to me after their mother's death. Also to Anne for helping to trace family.

To the Harley Gallery at Welbeck for their friendly assistance in accessing Derek Adlam's book *Tunnel Vision* from which I was able to put names to people and places.

For an unknown source of a small booklet, which unfortunately we have not been able to trace. From this we were able to put a few details to the stories we had heard of the eccentric 5th Duke's buildings.

To Austin Macauley for their welcome advice and most importantly, for publishing my book.

To all my family for their support and encouragement in the writing of this book.

In particular, my special thanks to my brilliant daughter in law, Shelly Pogson, for her time and efforts in researching census and other details and for patiently guiding me through modern technology!

Preface

If one reads the D.H. Lawrence novel, *Women in Love*, one comes across the following passage:

Winnie, the young daughter of the wealthy landowner Thomas Crich, asks her father if she can give a bouquet of flowers to her tutor Gudrun, who is returning from a time away in London.

Her father sends her to go and see Wilson the gardener and to tell him 'I say you are to have what you want'. Winnie goes round the greenhouses and conservatory choosing all the blooms she wants for the presentation bouquet.

'A presentation bouquet?' asks Wilson.

'Who's coming then? The Duchess of Portland?'

This then the story of the gardener who really did do the "Flowers for the Duchess".

Introduction
Flowers for the Duchess

James Pogson, my late father-in-law, was born in 1884 into an already large family.

In later years, after James died, we came across his working diary for 1911 together with numerous old photographs and mementoes from his and his family's time in service at Welbeck Abbey.

Piecing them together with stories he used to tell us, recalling those bygone times, I thought his life worthy of recording, a nostalgic insight of life in service.

Down the years a name perpetuated in this family has been James Pogson. This story is about the James born in 1884. James's family came into being when his father, another James, met and fell in love with a young girl, named Charlotte Chapel.

After a long courtship, they married and produced a large family, and were to spend nearly all their lives in service to the Duke and Duchess of Portland at Welbeck Abbey, situated in the Dukeries, Nottinghamshire. Charlotte, the girl James met, was born in the village of Weston, Notts, in 1844. At thirteen years of age, she went into service to a family in a neighbouring village. Having grown up in a large family herself, she was a very capable girl and proved to be a good servant. Her parents were grateful she had been found a place with a good family so near to home. She stayed in that situation for four years.

Then an opportunity for Charlotte came when she was offered a move into service with a prominent family, the Creightons, who lived in another local village. This was Ordsall in Notts. It was deemed a better position for her, so her parents persuaded her to take it. She settled into the new family life very well, was obviously well thought of, and so was happy in her new situation. Sometime during the six years of her service in Ordsall was when she met James. This could have been when he was working nearby, possibly in the village forge or in forestry. In this rural community, people would know of the local families, happenings and events by word of mouth.

Back in the 1860s we can only imagine how life was for Charlotte and James. Charlotte would only have a half day off each week, usually on Sunday, when she would go to see her family, except, of course, on Mothering Sunday, when she would be given the whole day off to spend with her mother and the family. Perhaps on these visits home she would be able to meet James. Generally they would not be able to spend much time together, no doubt the reason for a long courtship, which was quite common then. Another problem, of course, was the need to find somewhere to live once married. Girls would leave their place of service to settle down and become housewives and mothers. Charlotte and James were at last able to marry in November 1867. James was twenty-eight and Charlotte was twenty-three.

James was born in 1839 in the village of Bothamsol. This was one of a cluster of villages, including Weston and Whitwell, in the Nottingham Forest area, centred on the town of Worksop. The area was also known as the Dukeries, which we read of later.

As with many rural communities, the main employment for men was as agricultural workers, woodmen or blacksmiths. So much of what was needed and used was made in the forges, especially the shoeing of horses, of which there were many. They were used on the land, in the forest and at the local coal mines. There were several collieries around Worksop.

James took whatever employment was offered but he became skilled as a woodman, and it was the work he most enjoyed. He was much happier working outside. The Nottingham Forest was far reaching and provided plenty of work in the continual round of maintenance as trees were felled to provide wood for many purposes, including pit props. Work could be had working in the mines but this depended on how near you lived to the nearest one. To have to walk four or five miles at either end of a day working down the pit was not a happy choice.

For villagers, the highlight of the week was travelling into Worksop on Saturdays, on the horse-drawn carts. The stalls were plentiful with a wide variety of wares. The farmers' wives brought in their dairy produce and eggs. There was crockery, pots and pans, shoes and boots, haberdashery, nearly everything which was needed.

You would not be looking forward to the journey in if you were suffering toothache! A 'tooth puller' used to practice at the Worksop market.

The poor patient would sit on a chair while the offending tooth would be pulled out with a pair of plier-like tongs, no anaesthetic, and everyone looking on! It must have been horrendous. It all conjures up a very colourful scene. Perhaps it was on one of these Saturdays James met Charlotte. We do not know.

On the occasion of their marriage, the Creighton family presented Charlotte with a Bible. It is inscribed thus:

Presented to Charlotte Chapel by Eliza, Arthur and C. Creighton as a marriage token of her faithful service in their family during six years. Ordshall 25th November 1867.

As partners of the grace of life
May you each other's burden bear
May mutual love exclude all Strife
And Kindness banish every care.
Thus blest and happy may you live
And when you're called by death away
The wreck of time may you survive
And reign with God in endless day

Opposite this inscription and the verses is given the following collect.

Blessed Lord, who has caused all Holy scriptures to be written for our learning, grant that we may in such wise hear them, read, mark, learn and inwardly digest them that by patience and comfort of the Word, we may embrace and ever hold fast the blessed hope of everlasting life which thou hast given us in our saviour Jesus Christ. Amen.

We do not know if the Creightons were a clergy family. They were obviously religious and trusted their writings would give guidance for faith. We are told a Bible was sometimes the only means of teaching children to read. At that time education was not compulsory but unlike many other rural children, Charlotte could read and write. She was to use this Bible well; each child she bore was faithfully recorded in it (as was her marriage to James on 25th November)

George	1868
Elizabeth	1870
Mary	1872
Harry	1874
Sarry	1875
Arthur	1877
James and Marther	1879
Florence	1881
Hannah and Gertrude	1883

James	1884
Ernest	1886
Edgar	1888

From records available, we find their first three children were born in Charlotte's home village of Weston. George was her firstborn in December 1868, the year after her marriage. Charlotte was delighted with her new little son. He was baptised at St. Mary Priory Church. As was usual in those days, before a child was baptised the new mother would be 'churched'. She would attend her church for a service known as the churching of women, when thanks would be given for the safe delivery of a child.

During her lifetime, Charlotte would be 'churched' many times. She knew she was fortunate in all her babies being safely delivered but would grieve when four of those babies died in infancy.

As George grew, he was quite often out with his father, who was working in the large wooded areas on the estate. However, nearing twenty years of age, he must have contracted consumption, rife at that time. He succumbed to the disease and after a short illness, died. His sister Elizabeth was born in 1870. She was a lively girl and a great help to Charlotte as she got older and the family increased. Briefly working in service, she married by the time she was twenty and lived to the grand old age of a hundred and three. She obviously had what was known then as a strong constitution! She was still bustling around, looking after her own little home and making pound after pound of marmalade for church funds.

The blessing for all children born at this time was the new Education Act which came into force. It would mean all the Pogson children had the benefit of attending school.

Mary Anne arrived in 1972. She was always known as Polly. She loved her older sister, trying to do everything Elizabeth did. This worked well for them when they were older. Together they went into service away from the Abbey into the home of Joseph Ashton, a mining engineer.

Sometime after these three children had been born the family moved to Bothamsol, which was James's home village. We can only assume a better chance of work and accommodation presented itself. Shortly after their arrival in Bothamsol, another son, Harry, was born, in 1874. Like most of the menfolk in the family, when older, Harry would also work on the estate. We think he was around thirty years of age when he married a girl named Annie from the neighbouring village of Whitwell. He had been fortunate to acquire a cottage very near the estate.

We notice so many did not marry before they were thirty or more and that was after fairly long courtships. This, we think, was the problem of finding somewhere in the area to live and set up home.

After Harry's birth the life-changing opportunity arose for the family.

James obtained a permanent position at Welbeck Abbey. Welbeck was the country estate of the Dukes of Portland, situated in 'The Dukeries' in North Nottinghamshire; it was said to be the largest country estate at that time.

The area became known as the Dukeries because five aristocratic families established their country homes there. Together with Welbeck, they were Clumber Park, Rufford Abbey, Thoresby Park and Newstead Abbey (Lord Byron's home).

The 5th Duke of Portland was the second of four sons of the 4th Duke, but in 1824 his elder brother died unexpectedly. He therefore became the heir. He soon became known as a very eccentric character. Many stories have been told of his strange behaviour and lifestyle. The Duke never married. The love of his life was Adelaide Kemble[1], a famous English operatic singer, but sadly for the Duke she was already married. Her marriage was kept secret because of her career.

---

[1] From Derek Adlam's Book, *Tunnel Vision*

The poor Duke was unaware of this situation until she had to turn down his proposal of marriage and explain. He never considered marrying anyone else.

Thereafter, he became obsessed with building works at the Abbey. The new riding house he built was the second largest in the world, with only the huge manège next to the Kremlin[2] in Moscow being larger. The 'Tan Gallop'[3] was two furlongs long for the training of racehorses. The Duke's most famous project was the building of the underground tunnels. These two and half miles of underground drives were wide enough for two horse-drawn carriages to pass side by side. Plate glass skylights and gas lamps gave the lighting. He was reluctant that people should know his business so these tunnels enabled him to travel to and from Welbeck in secrecy.

When he was leaving the Abbey, his carriage would drive through the tunnels and emerge at South Lodge. From there, it would soon cover the few miles to Worksop station. There the curtained carriage, with the Duke still inside, would be loaded onto the private train for the journey to London. Servants were instructed not to acknowledge him unless he engaged them in conversation. His strange behaviour gave rise to stories and questions. Many people believed he was living a double life as a family man, as the journeys to London were very frequent. His London home was surrounded by high walls, which again indicated great secrecy. We shall never know.

So, James went into service at Welbeck in 1875, four years before the 5th Duke died, and in that time became well aware of his eccentricity. Stories filtered down the years of his strange behaviour.

They were given the occupancy of South Lodge on the estate. Charlotte in particular was very relieved and thankful to move into their own home with the growing family. George

---

[2] Ibid.
[3] Ibid.

was now six, Elizabeth four, Polly two and Harry a baby. They now had the wonderful benefit of six rooms.

The Lodge was situated at the tunnel entrance which gave access to the main road to Worksop, where the nearest railway station was. Charlotte was required to open and shut the gates for conveyances passing through. This would, of course, include the ducal family as well as the daily carriers bringing in supplies and the daily visits of the postman in his pony and trap. In later years, her daughters at home would help her in this duty. Shortly after moving into the Lodge another daughter, Sarah, was born. At thirteen years of age, she would go into service at the Abbey, starting as a general help. This meant getting up early, cleaning the fire grates and laying the fires. The footman would have carried the coals up and down the backstairs. Then Sarah would take hot water round to the bedrooms. Over the years, she proved herself an amiable and conscientious servant and gradually made her way up the placing in the Abbey staff, eventually becoming lady's maid to the Duchess.

Arthur, another son, was born in 1877.

The baby survived for just one year. He died in May 1878. James and Charlotte were to suffer grief again when twins were born in 1879. A daughter, Marther, (as written in the Bible), was named for her grandmother but only lived for sixteen months. Her twin, a son, was named James after his father but he too died, at eighteen months. It must have been heartbreaking to have these last three children for such a short time and then to lose them.

Many children and young adults died during these years. Consumption and infant illnesses were common. There was no provision, especially in rural areas, to quarantine and treat these infections. People had to try and cope with their homemade potions and remedies but they nearly all proved to be ineffective, of course. For many, malnutrition was another cause, but there was no question of that problem here. The employees at Welbeck were well catered for with provision made for them, especially with everything which was produced on the estate. Vegetables, meat and milk from the home farm and coal from the mine at Welbeck.

Father-in-law always told us how good life was for them.

After the sad loss of their three babies, Charlotte once again conceived. There seems to have been some concern over the coming birth. Her mother, Elizabeth, moved into South Lodge to be with her when the baby was born. To make room for her stay it was decided that the little ten-year-old Elizabeth would go and live with her grandfather Samuel and the family in Weston.

The baby, Florence, was born safely in 1881 but she was always a sickly child. We can see reference to her poor health in one of the notes the Duchess wrote to father-in-law. However, she survived until she was thirty years of age, but of course never married.

Twin girls arrived next in 1883, named Hannah and Gertrude. Sadly, Hannah was to live for only thirteen months but Gertrude survived. She thrived and lived at home until she married late in life. These large families were not unusual in the Victorian era. They were the result of couples not having the knowledge and benefit of birth control. Thankfully we know James and Charlotte were happy with their children and grieved for the ones they lost.

On the Duke's death in 1879 the dukedom and estate passed to a cousin, as neither of his younger brothers had married and both died before him.

So, the new 6th Duke acceded to the title. This was the twenty-one-year-old William Cavendish Bentinck KG, first cousin once removed. Both the 5th and 6th Dukes were descended from the 3rd Duke. The cousins had never met.

Born and living in Perthshire, the new Duke had never visited Welbeck.

As yet unmarried, when he arrived at the Abbey he was accompanied by his step-mother, Lady Rosebery, and family, which included his half-sister Lady Ottoline Morell. A lady about whom much has been written! They helped him settle into his new domain and position. He was said to be always very grateful for Lady Rosebery's advice with many of the situations which arose, especially with organising services again after the 5th Duke's demolition of the private chapel, as we shall read later.

Ten years later, in 1889, William married the beautiful Winifred Dallas-Yorke, who also originated from Perthshire. They most probably knew each other well before he inherited the dukedom.

The new Duchess arrived at Welbeck and, after the cheerless days of the eccentric, bachelor Duke, the whole lifestyle of the estate changed. She soon made the effort to meet all the staff and servants and took an interest in their lives and welfare. The Duke started to organise the structure and activities to his preference and created better working conditions.

Unlike his predecessor, he was fulfilling duties in the country and the county both with official and social occasions. Charlotte and James, together with all who worked at Welbeck, welcomed the more relaxed atmosphere which now came over the place.

Then the James I write about was born in 1884, and we shall read of his time at Welbeck. As he grew older, he was often called Jim to avoid confusion with his father.

His younger brother, Ernest, was born in 1886 and finally the last child, Edgar, in 1888.

This was to be another year of mixed emotions as it was the year in which George, Charlotte's first child, died. For one son to be born and another son to die within such a short space of time must have been difficult to cope with. The joy of a baptism and the grief of a funeral.

Young James was four years old at the time.

He had no memory of this older brother George or of his death and funeral. However, he did have a vague recollection of a new baby arriving in the Lodge.

These three youngest boys all entered service on the estate.

In 1897, when James was thirteen, he went into the bothy to become a gardening boy, along with the other lads working in the gardens. The bothy was where these young boys lived while in training. This enabled them to be up and about early for their various duties under the supervision of the estate gardeners.

The 1901 census is headed by the Duke and Duchess and shows all those in service in the Abbey and living on the estate.

Life was probably a little crowded in South Lodge; we see Gertrude, eighteen, and James, seventeen, Ernest is fifteen, Edgar thirteen.

With the six, now grown up, children at home we can only imagine how busy Charlotte must have been with all the cleaning, washing and cooking for the eight of them to be dealt with every day. Gertrude would no doubt help with all the chores with Florence coping with the lighter jobs. All of this without any of the appliances which we take for granted nowadays. They did not have the benefit of electricity. Cooking was done on the kitchen range which needed nonstop attention and raking coals which created plenty of dust. Ironing could only be done when there was no cooking in progress. The flat irons would be heated on the range and would need to be wiped off before use.

Lighting was by paraffin lamps which needed to be trimmed and filled each day. The effects of these lamps caused their own problems. Materials and paper became discoloured, as we can see from the Bible and other items we have.

Ernest had followed James into the bothy two years later. Both boys were by now working in the gardens but often recalled their time in the bothy when, as one might expect, the lads all together in there made their own fun and got up to the usual pranks when the opportunity arose! In 1911, an espalier fruit tree was planted, which still thrives today. Whenever we looked at it in later years, and at the date plaque fixed to the wall against it, we wondered if James and Ernest had helped with its planting and nurture. They were to become good gardeners.

With his brothers working in the gardens, Edgar now started his working life in the forge, which he enjoyed. A nonstop round of shoeing the many horses working around the grounds, the thoroughbred horses used for riding and the hunters which were prized animals.

The three brothers became very close as they grew older, especially with working so close together.

They would often see each other during their working day. James and Ernest enjoyed working in the gardens and in the many glasshouses where exotic plants, fruit and flowers were grown. James went on to tend the impressive palm house, the camellia house and the endless array of flowering plants which were used in the floral arrangements in the Abbey.

Thus, he gradually became involved with the Abbey. The family's lives during the first decade in the century appear to have been spent contentedly living and serving in their various duties.

These were always referred to as the golden years at Welbeck. The Duke and Duchess had become the proud parents of three children; Lady Victoria, born in 1890, a son who became the Marquis of Titchfield, born in 1893, and a second son, Lord Francis, born in 1900.

The social life for the ducal family was very full. We can see reference in James's diary to house parties, events and guests at the Abbey. There is mention of society life in London and the shooting season in Scotland. Also, Lady Victoria's coming of age celebration.

We also read of the Abbey staff performing in the choir and choral society and exhibiting Welbeck produce at York horticultural show.

It was a good time to be at Welbeck. The servants were well cared for and they were particularly fond of the Duchess, who made sure all was well with them. Stories were recounted of the servants' dances which the Duchess arranged for them, held in the underground ballroom. They all had great fun dancing the lancers and quadrilles. A dance in particular which caused much merriment was when small circles were formed. The men would go as fast as they could, trying to lift the girls off their feet! Perhaps it was at one of these dances that James would meet Edith and Ernest would meet Annie, who were housemaids in the Abbey.

It was during this time James's diary was kept. Sometime before 1911 he had become established in his position and was given his own, very small, dwelling, as we can see from the 1911 census. He also had his garden room in the Abbey, where he worked and tended his plants and flowers and assembled his floral decorations. He had become known for his love and artistry of flowers. From notes the Duchess sent him we realise how gifted and creative he was. For one grand occasion, he designed a small stream running the full length of the table through a central arrangement of greenery and small flowers. We still have the mechanics of this beautiful table. However, he was always very modest about his work. It was usually other people who told us of his talents.

This then, the contents of the diary. They give us an insight, not just to flowers, but to certain aspects of life at Welbeck. In those days of course, the diary was all written in pencil, which is sometimes difficult to decipher. Also, not being too well versed with logistics and other terms used about the flowers, I have copied it to the best of my ability. I think it makes interesting reading.

By then, at twenty-eight years of age, he was doing most of the floristry in the Abbey.

The diary shows that January was a quiet month. The Duke and Duchess had probably stayed on in their London home after the Christmas celebration.

Only three entries are made, each noting the flowers he used in the glass vases in the Duchess's dressing room; white lilac at first, then amaryllis, and toward the end of the month, pink camellias.

It would appear there were visitors at the Abbey during February. We can see reference to the Duke and Duchess's daughter, Lady Victoria, celebrating her twenty-first birthday then.

February 25th	For the dining table Vermillion brilliant Long fourteen top. I can only assume this refers to the number of guests on the long- or top- table.
February 26th	Pink hyacinths (Gertrude) for the dining table. Again, fourteen long top.
February 27th	The company cleared out after luncheon. Presentation to Lady Victoria in the underground ballroom
February 28th	For the table, pink camellias, one cross piece. Looked very well. A social was held at wood yard to which I went.
March 1st	Golden spur daffodils for the table
March 3rd	Table – tulips Van de Neer? and white ones N.B. Rabjohn went to Rugby to see Mrs Arthur James about situation in Holland
March 4th	Table – Empress daffodils. Small glasses
March 5th	Table – Jonquils 10 small glasses
March 6th	Table – Tulips. Cottage maid and white ones. One bowl and 6 small glasses. 10 top

March 7th	Table – Empress daffodils
March 8th	Table – Hyacinths pink (Gertrude). 2 curved glasses and 7 small ones
March 9th	Table – Jonquils 10 small glasses 8 on top. 6 ladies and 2 gents.
March 10th	The Duchess went to London for dinner Table – Tulips Josephine and white ones.
March 11th	The Duke and Countesses went to London. Miss Morton left. (We can only surmise these were the four people for dinner on the 10th but do not know who the Countesses and Miss Morton were). N.B. Rabjohn also went to London on the 2.12 pm train – (perhaps to take flowers down for use there)
March 12th	Cleared the flower glasses out of all the rooms (the staff probably now having a break from fulltime attendance). I sent a letter to Rabjohn relating to the Holland situation. (Was Rabjohn looking for new situation? At this stage he was planning to get married later in the year).
March 13th	Cleared out all the plants except the big ones. Rabjohn went to Holland from London via Harwich

March 14th	Started to pot plumbago in the corridor. Storm of hail and snow. Very cold.
March 15th	Changed the Eucalyptus in the gothic hall and the cypresses in the boudoir. Storm of hail and snow again. The Duke went to Glengarry from London.
March 16th	Started to put the groups in the gothic hall after dinner. Rabjohn came back by the 9.18 train. I went to meet him with his bicycle. Storms of hail and snow continue.
March 17th	Finished all the groups off and boxed all in.
March 18th	The Duchess came back after lunch. 7 for dinner used pink camellias with eucalyptus in the Duchess's dressing room. Table – Narcissus Incomparabilis
March 19th	Flowers for lunch tulips Dere von Thal. Dinner Table – tulips pink beauty 8 or 10 top
March 20th	Let one fire out in corridor (the fires were used to keep the plants warm in cold weather) potted plumbago in corridor. Table centre prunus and six small glasses of daffodils. 10 top. 5 ladies and 4 gentlemen.

March 21st	Lunch table. Hyacinths, Pink corregio, potted denara Table dinner. Tulips Dere van Thal. 4 quarter crescent glasses and 3 small glasses 10 top.
March 22nd	The Duchess went to London Dinner table cyclamen. Just 4 for dinner.
March 23rd	Miss Morton here alone. No dinner.
March 24th	The Duchess came back from London Used imentophyllium with eucalyptus and cornus in the Duchess's dressing room. No dinner
March 25th	Dinner table tulips cottage maid. (Visitors must have arrived again as he notes 8 on top/table)
March 26th	Dinner table daffodils Emperor 8 on 10 top.
March 27th	Rabjohn to London
March 28th	Dinner table cyclamen just 4 for dinner.
March 29th	Put Rhododendron Pink Peach in cradle on large table. Pyrus on small table with eucalyptus, pyrus with compressus in the coffer (or copper?) [sic] Table tulips Gesneriana, lutea (yellow) 4 for dinner

March 30th	Miss Morton went away Rabjohn came back 1.15 at Worksop. Put amaryllis in the boudoir. White lilac in the Duchess's bedroom. Dinner table Primula obconica (German primrose) 2 for dinner
March 31st	Used imentophylliums again in the Duchess's dressing room glasses Dinner table – Emperor daffodils 3 for dinner

We keep seeing references to Rabjohn. It is thought he was on the domestic gardening staff and assisted with the plants and flowers, primarily in the glass houses and conservatory. We assume it is Rabjohn with James in two of the photographs. He was obviously looking for another situation as he was getting married in the near future and needed to find a position with living accommodation to start a home with his new wife.

April 2nd	Attended service in Chapel. Rabjohn's and H. Johnson's Banns were published for the first time Used daffodils Balli compicuos? For dining table just the Duke and Duchess for dinner

April 3rd	The Duchess went to London by the 6.30 train. Thrushes nest in the Bachelors' Hall with 3 eggs in. Emperor daffodils for the dinner table. 3 for dinner
April 4th	Used azalea mollis with eucalyptus and cornus in the Duchess's dressing room For the dinner table cottage maid tulips 2 for dinner.
April 5th	Several snowstorms during the day and very cold went to practice (choir?) and service Dinner table Emperor daffodils and flowers of pyrus japonica on the cloth.
April 6th	Sharp frost 10 degrees Table narcissus
April 7th	Got in some kerria from the rose garden for using with carnations in the Duchess's dressing room. Present at choir practice in Church. Dinner table. Tulips and rose lusiante 3 for dinner
April 8th	Changed the lilac in the coppers in the music room Table prunus 4 for dinner
April 9th Palm Sunday	Attended service Lunch table prunus and daffodils Dinner table azalea Mollis 4 for dinner

April 10th	Used Mrs Burnett carnations in the Duchess's dressing room glasses Arranged magnolia speciora in the cradle and took out Rhododrendons. Dinner table rose Grisdelin? and tulips. 1 bowl and 4 small glasses
April 11th	Present at practice for choral society Lenni magnolia and azalea in the bedrooms Dinner table emperor daffodils
April 12th	Present at practice and service in the chapel Dinner table yellow tulips
April 13th	Changed the plants in the cradle. Took out magnolia speciora and put in rhododendrons. Changed the eucalyptus in the boudoir table. Prunus for centre and Emperor daffodils from outside.
April 14th	Went to service in chapel and practice after
Good Friday	Changed the vases in the Duchess's dressing room. Used Mrs Burnett carnations again. Dinner table pyrus floribunda and yellow tulips
Easter Sunday April 16th	Dinner table daffodils minimus? From the new drive and prunus prisadi
April 17th	Table magnolia lenni

April 18th	Rabjohn left 7 o'clock. Johnston came in half past two. (Was this Rabjohn's successor?) The Duke went away by the 2.12 train The Duchess and Lady Victoria by 7.15 train No dinner. Went to church practice
April 19th	Cleared out the large plants in the gothic hall and from the house library Rabjohn was married today in Scotland.
April 20th	Put the big plants back in again in the evening.
April 21st	Present at Church and choir practice
April 22nd	Frank Brown left here at 1.30 for Newmarket Dinner table daffodils
April 23rd	Only the Duke for dinner. Wild cherry for table
April 24th	Choral practice in underground rooms. Table Emperor daffodils 4 for dinner
April 25th	Choral society concert in underground rooms very successful Table empress daffodils and Pyrus Japonica on the cloth. 8 top
April 26th	Table azalea 10 top
April 27th	Table small daffodils and small tulips with snowy mispilar? One centre piece

April 28th	Went to the Sheffield music festival by the 5.15 Train Table narcissus pactires? 10 top 9 Glasses
April 29th	Dinner table double wild cherry, narcissus imcomparatis and amelanchis 13 on 15 top
April 30th	Table daffodil incomparatis 10 top
May 1st	Table tulips Clara Butt 8 top
May 2nd	Went to the Retford (music) competition won in each class 4 firsts. The Duchess and house party came over for concert in the evening Mrs Rubens (soprano) staying at the Abbey Table empress daffodils 10 top

It would appear that after their short break away after Easter, the Duke and Duchess held a house party from 25th April until 3rd May. This because of the musical events. The choir were all members of staff at the Abbey.

May 5th	The Duke and Duchess were to go to London today but Lady Victoria got German measles so did not go. Just their graces for dinner Table pink roses – Mrs Laing

May 6th	Changed the large group of plants in the cradle in the gothic hall Table wild cherry
May 7th	Table scarlet Geraniums
May 20th	The Duke went to London alone. Her Grace and Lord Francis here (their younger son)
May 24th	The Duchess went to London by the 6.55 train from Retford

As there are no more entries until 13th June we can only assume their graces were staying in London.

June 13th	Went to the York show with Gibson and J. Hay by the 3.26 train from Retford
14th	1st prize with decorated fruit table and two collections of fruit and 1st with the collection of vegetables. Came back with Gibson on 6.58
June 15th	J. Hay came back from the York show
June 16th	I went back to York to pack up the fruit and vegetables. Got back on the 6.50 train

Horticultural shows were very popular, especially in the north and the gardening staff at Welbeck usually entered flowers and vegetables from the estate.

June 24th	Their Graces and B. Carr arrived Dinner table red and white sweet peas
June 25th	Her Grace went away again at 6 o'clock Table pink roses in white and gilt basket.
June 26th	B. Carr went away 10 o'clock His Grace went away by the 2.12 train
July 8th	His Grace and B. Carr came in to dinner
July 9th	Table red and white sweet peas. 2 for dinner
July 10th	Table roses Sharman Crawford? 8 on 10 top
July 11th	Her Grace went away. The Anglo German automobile club came here for lunch in the picture gallery 3 18 top tables 1 Mrs Burnett Malmaison, 1 white and dark red and 1 blush Malmaison 8 ice pails on the long table down side 5 for dinner at night.

We think 'B. Carr' was organising this event with the Duke.

| July 12th | His Grace went to London by the 2.12 train cleared all the cut flowers out in the afternoon |
| July 13th | Went to London by the 8.39 from Worksop for the choir trip. Went to see the exhibition at the Crystal Palace and to the White City and came back by the 11.50 |

Their Graces were up in London preparing for a Ball

July 20th	Went to 3 Grosvenor Square for the Ball. Took Grant up with me. 3 tables for dinner 2 done with Blush Malmaison and 1 with Princess of Wales. 2x16's and 1x12 supper table Malmaison.
July 21st	Came back from London by the 7.15 Brought back the empties Miss Morton came down by the same train.
July 22nd	The Duke came back and Baker Carr 3 for dinner
July 24th	The Duchess came back Dinner table Princess of Wales Malmaison
July 25th	Table sweet peas
July 26th	Table Sharman Crawford roses
July 27th	Table Blush Malmaison

July 28th	His Grace dined 7.30 Table pink and white sweet peas
July 29th	Table Caroline? Testout roses
July 30th	29 for dinner. The officers from the S. Rangers Camp came in Table Princess of Wales Malmaison
July 31st	Table sweet peas pink and white 6 on 8 top
Aug 2nd	10 for dinner on twelve top Hiawatha rose looks excellent at night one of the best
Aug 3rd	Table Caroline Testout roses
Aug 4th	Table sweet peas 7 on 8 top
Aug 5th	The show party came in. 31 for dinner 2 sixteens Table Richmond roses and lily of the valley. The table did not look as well as it might have done as the roses were not up to the standard. Many of them being in the bunch 32 dozen roses and 10 dozen bunches of lily of the valley (bought Page)
Aug 6th	Lunch 2 jardin and 1 sugar bowl Richmond roses 2 round tables for dinner 32 Dinner tables may day carnations (pink) 32 dozen bought (Page)

Aug 7th bank holiday	Did the riding school with green on Tapling? and sweet peas for the show luncheon, looked very well Dinner tables Caroline Testout 31 for dinner
Aug 8th	Dinner table scarlet geraniums and maidenhair fern. 21 on long table
Aug 9th	Table sweet peas pink and white the best one we have done 16 top
Aug 10th	Table Mrs Sharman Crawford roses 12 for dinner
Aug 15th	His Grace and servants leave for Scotland

The shooting season started on the 12th and the Portlands and a large number of staff moved up to their estate in Scotland. During their time away from Welbeck, the remaining staff were able to take their holidays.

Aug 16th	Mrs Dallas Yorke (the Duchess's Mother) came to stay a few weeks with her Grace until the Duchess left for Scotland on the 29th.

The Duchess must have delayed her journey up to Scotland to arrange this visit from her mother.

Between 2nd September and 23rd September the gardening staff took it in turns for their holiday.

Sep 28th	Harvest festival at Welbeck Plants used – Friday. Cupresses macrocarpa geraniums lilium tiger and autumn foliage. Finished early today on account of services.
Sep 29th	Harvest festival services 8 o'clock and 7 pm
Oct 2nd	Cleared the plants out of the Chapel
Oct 8th	Went to the St. Cuthbert College at 3 o'clock to practice for opening of new Chapel
Oct 9th	Sent 12 small glasses to her Grace at Langwell
Oct 12th	Went with the dray to get moss, slipped when getting off the dray to open the ornamental gates, the front wheel going over both my knees. No bones broken.
Oct 13th	My legs not so stiff as expected Able to get about.
Oct 15th	Went to St. Cuthbert to practice
Oct 20th	Put the large plants in the Abbey Her Grace is in Edinburgh for the weekend
Oct 21st	Put the groups up in the Great Hall and Library

Oct 23rd	Her Grace and sister Grace arrived. Put the plants in the balcony and boxed in. Finished the other rooms off
Oct 24th	His Grace and servants came back from Scotland Arrived here about half past eight 16 Doz carnations came in, violets and lily of the valley. 14 for dinner, not so many as expected. Table carnations and lily.
Oct 25th	I went out to the shooting lunch The ladies went out. 16 Doz Richmond roses, the same of Source d'or chrysanths and 4 Doz Sunbeam chrysanths came in – very good lot 14 top Table – Richmond roses and lily of the valley
Oct 26th	Went out to the shooting lunch. The ladies came out. Rained very heavily so did not shoot after lunch. Dinner table Mrs Burnett carnations 14 top
Oct 27th	Went out to shooting lunch Dinner table chrysanths Source d'or and the best of the autumn foliage

Oct 28th	I did not go to the shooting lunch Table scarlet geraniums and maidenhair fern 17 on long table
Oct 29th	Table lilium 17 on long table
Oct 30th	Table Kary thistledome chrysanths Table 10 long.
Oct 31st	Table Salvia splendens table 8 top
Nov 1st	Table tropedium 8 top
Nov 2nd	Mary Richardson chrysanths 8 top
Nov 5th	The Duke and Duchess and Lady Victoria went to London then onto Flete (Mildmays)
Nov 9th	Her Grace came back
Nov 10th	The Duke and Lady Victoria came back
Nov 12th	Her Grace went to Newcastle and then onto Underly Hall
Nov 13th	His Grace went to Underly Hall Lady Victoria and B. Carr went away
Nov 16th	Lady Victoria came in unexpected Had her rooms to do after she arrived
Nov 17th	The Duke and Duchess came back. Table Lady Congress chrysanths

Nov 20th	The Duke and Duchess and Lady Victoria went to Belvoir Castle (home of the Dukes of Rutland)
Nov 21st	Took the big eucalyptus out of the gothic hall and phormiums out of the front hall
Nov 23rd	Put the eucalyptus and phormiums back in the front hall
Nov 24th	Miss Morton came in Changed the copper in the gothic hall

Apart from the flowers noted, there would have been lots of greenery involved. This was always his style of arrangement.

There are no more entries in the diary. Perhaps because James and helpers were busy with the preparation for the festive decorations for both Abbey and for the temporary chapel.

He must have been very busy just before the thirteenth of December when it would seem there was an important dinner at the Abbey.

One of the Duchess's crested notes which she sent to him was for this occasion:

Pogson – the dinner table was beautiful last night. The most artistic colouring and arrangements I ever saw, and know what a long time it must have taken you – and what labour and thought!

Another, undated, asks him to put a few more flowers especially in the little library today – as a foreign lady is coming for the night and I want the rooms to look nice.

Could this have been Queen Ena of Spain, who we know visited the Abbey around that time?

Of course, by this time Sarah had become lady's maid to the Duchess, whom she adored. Sarah never married and was in service until she died at the age of fifty-five. The Duchess was said to be deeply saddened at Sarah's death. In recognition of her faithful service, she gave the money for a headstone for Sarah in Worksop Cemetery. We saw this headstone in later years but now all headstones have been removed.

Sarah would have been with the Duchess when James was working in the Abbey. We like to think they would see each other very often.

So life went on. The living in the Lodge was more settled by 1911.

Fortunately, sometime during this year a formal photograph was taken of the now adult family; only Elizabeth is missing from it. She was now married and living near Sheffield with her new husband. Polly would soon be leaving home to be married. It would be the last photograph they had all together and would always be treasured. At least by now, contact between family and friends had become much improved, especially for those in service, who often moved about with their employers for the seasons during the year. Postcards had become a popular way of keeping in touch. They were plentiful, cheap to send and promptly delivered. We find it most interesting to look through a small collection which we have. The messages sent do not give much information, unfortunately, just 'Arrived safely', 'the parcel has arrived', 'going home Tues', etc.

During 1913 work started on the building of a new church for Welbeck. When the 6th Duke inherited the title and moved into the Abbey, he discovered his eccentric predecessor had demolished the private chapel. As Welbeck was extra-parochial, there was no parish church to attend. Initially services were held in the underground ballroom and later in a curtained-off area of the old riding school. A temporary chapel made of corrugated iron had been erected in 1890.

A choir was formed from the young men and the boys from the estate. James, Ernest and Edgar all sang in the choir, as we see from the diary. The Duke decided a proper church should be built and the work commenced, although it took much longer than hoped, as we shall read later. These must have been the easiest and most contented years for Charlotte and James Snr., their surviving children now all grown to adulthood. But from the time of the family photograph, the forthcoming years were to dramatically change their lives forever.

Within twelve months, Florence's health deteriorated quite quickly and she sadly died before the year was out. She was just thirty-one years of age.

And then the momentous year of 1914 arrived. It became a year of mixed emotions on the estate. Welbeck was 'en fete' for the celebrations to mark the silver wedding anniversary of the Duke and Duchess, and also the coming of age of their eldest son, the Marquis of Titchfield. The estate workers were kept busy preparing for the event, which was on the 12th of June.

The clouds hanging over the forthcoming event were the situation in Europe and, for the Pogson family, James Snr.'s health. He was weakened with illness and sadly died just two years after Florence had died.

Then came the Great War; life changed for everyone.

Gradually the younger men on the estate volunteered for the Army. For the boys in that area, most would enlist with Sherwood Foresters.

Edgar was one of the first to volunteer, soon followed by Ernest. With quite a number of the young gardeners leaving to fight, it was decided James should stay on at the Abbey to join in with the vegetable and fruit production. Edith, the housemaid mentioned earlier, was courting James, but she enlisted to join the Women's Flying Corps, as it was then known, before being founded as the Royal Air Force.

With his brothers away at war and his father having recently died, James was now his mother's main support. We think he moved back into the Lodge to be with her. Everyone was striving hard to keep the estate maintained and life for everyone was difficult. We know from all that has been written, how distressing it must have been for the families whose boys were fighting over in France. Over time news would come through of another loss of a Welbeck boy. In all, twenty were to lose their lives.

Edgar was to spend all of his war in France. We believe he only came home once during all that time and only then because he was wounded in 1916. His mother must have been overjoyed to see him, especially with his father having died.

Ernest was not sent over to France; he remained in England, in an Army depot, so did not experience the fighting and desolation.

After Edgar returned to duty he was put in the transport section. We have a newspaper cutting from the following year, announcing he had been awarded the Military Medal.

It was whilst serving in transport that he earned the distinction. In a letter to his mother he says, 'I have got the Military Medal for getting rations up to the line under heavy shell fire. Two of us on the transport got it. We were the only transport to get through in the brigade for two nights.'

Reading the Sherwood Foresters war diary, this was during the Battle of Messines, getting supplies up to the Scottish lines. This occurred during the seventh to the tenth of June, 1917.

On the sixth of June, the awards of the two MM'S were posted to M. Dunn and E. Pogson.

Then in 1918, Edgar was engaged in one of the last battles of the War, from the fourth to the seventh of October, at Guisancourt farm. This was a strongly defended area in a line of attack.

The fighting appears to have been fierce over four days, with numbers of men from both sides killed and badly wounded. Sadly, Edgar was one of those seriously wounded and he did not survive. He died on the seventh of October.

The suffering for his mother and his family must have been heartbreaking.

In later years, I was able to visit his grave in Tincourt New British Cemetery, built to cope with all the casualties of this last battle. To see all those headstones and citations made one realise just what hell these boys, Edgar and his comrades in that battle, must have gone through and the grief which had been endured by their loved ones back home.

The church I wrote of earlier was finally completed by the end of the war. When the new lectern was installed, it had the names of Edgar and the other nineteen boys from the estate who had died in the war, engraved on it.

This was the commemoration to them.

The church was dedicated as St. Winifred's Church, Woodhouse Hall.

During the war, life was subdued with the depressing news which came from the front. The Duchess tried to keep as cheerful a presence as possible. Although hospitability could not be given as it has been previously, a certain amount of entertaining was able to be held.

The third crested note from the Duchess to James is dated 1st January 1916 and relates to a dinner on New Year's Eve.

Pogson – The dinner table was lovely last night. I did admire it so and especially the rosemary. I love rosemary and send you a piece as a remembrance of the pretty table.

A very thoughtful gesture, knowing rosemary is for remembrance. Perhaps to raise spirits, being aware how anxious the Pogson family were with Edgar so involved in the fighting.

Peace was finally declared in 1918. There was great rejoicing for many but also great sadness for lost loved ones.

Life on the estate was never the same again; with depleted numbers of staff and servants the previous lifestyle could not be maintained.

James continued with his work, tending plants in the conservatory and glasshouse and arranging flowers in the Abbey. He was more than relieved and pleased when Edith returned after her service in the Women's Flying Corps. By 1920 they were hoping to marry, but this would mean leaving Welbeck as they wanted to obtain their own independent home and living. James took a post offered to him with Sir Dennis Bailey at Lenton Abbey, Notts.

Ernest was fortunate to escape the fighting in France and so survive the war.

He was soon back working in the gardens, so thankful to have come through those awful years and be safely back at home. The beautiful herbaceous borders which he had tended before the war had all been dug out to provide land for growing vegetables. They were never to be restored to their former glory. James married Edith and had now left Welbeck for Lenton. Sometime in the early twenties Annie and Ernest were married. As they were the last of the family, they decided to settle into South Lodge to be with Charlotte. Unfortunately, they were never able to have children, due to an illness. Annie and Ernest cared for Charlotte until her death in 1927. She was so thankful she was able to stay in her home until the end of her days. In the years after the war, she had become more frail. Perhaps the loss of her husband at the start of the war, thus being on her own during the anxious years while Edgar was in France and then the tragedy of his death, affected her spirit. She must have felt how empty her life was in her old age after the full and busy life with all the family around the Lodge.

When one reflects on those years, we sense the joy of a young girl marrying her loved one. The births of their first children. Then coming with James and their small family to their new home when James entered service at Welbeck in 1875. It had been her home for fifty-two years. As the years went by came the arrival of more children, each carefully written in the family Bible. They had been content with the daily round, the friendship of other families living and serving on the estate. Sadly, they were also to suffer grief when they lost four of their infants; Arthur, the first James, Marther and Hannah the twins. Later in 1888, the year in which Charlotte gave birth to their last child, Edgar, their joy was overshadowed when their first born, George, died at twenty years of age.

Over the next two decades the three youngest boys were growing up and in turn taking up places of work at Welbeck. By 1911, when the family photograph was taken, they were all in their twenties and we see them as handsome young men. Their older brother is there with them, however by now he is married and 37 years old. It would be the last photograph taken of them together. Life was to change over the next few years.

Florence, smiling at the camera, had less than a year left to live. The family were desolate when she died. She was thirty-one years old. Charlotte and James sitting proudly with their grown-up family. They had been married for nearly forty-five years but more grief was to come when James died in 1914.

His death came during the preparation for the gala days to celebrate the silver wedding of the Duke and Duchess, together with the coming of age of the Marquis of Titchfield in June 1914, just before war was declared.

How poignant, especially to look at Edgar in the photo. Just twenty-three years of age, handsome, smart in his suit with watch chain. The 'baby' of the family. In a few short years, a willing volunteer when war was declared. Then, after four years surviving the terrible fighting he had been caught up in, to die so tragically just four weeks before peace was declared. One can only imagine his mother's grief. May Charlotte rest in peace with her loved ones.

Ernest and Annie would remain in South Lodge until the estate virtually closed up during the second war. The Army took over the Abbey in general. The Duke died there in 1943 and the Duchess in 1954. They had probably retained apartments there. After the war ended, the Abbey became a training college for army officers.

There is now a large garden centre there and the glasshouses still stand. Whether the glorious camellia house or the magnificent fruit arcade survived, which father-in-law talked of working in, I do not know.

The Harley Gallery is now established at Welbeck. It is many years since I last was able to visit, to see more of the Portland possessions.

We also visited St. Winifred's Church. The then Churchwarden's wife, Mrs Hester Thompson, showed us round and explained the history of the Church. Taking us into the Vestry we saw the large, framed photograph of the Choir which included the Pogson brothers. On the Lectern, we saw Edgar's name inscribed along with the other Welbeck boys who died in the First World War. We stood and thought of the sadness suffered by their families at Welbeck. Mrs Thompson also kindly sent me the booklet as shown in the Bibliography.

The Marquis of Titchfield acceded to the dukedom when his father died in 1943. He had married and moved into the newly built Woodhouse in 1932. He and the Marchioness had two daughters, Lady Anne and Lady Margaret. Lady Margaret married and had a son, William, who is now resident at the Abbey but I understand the title is now extinct.

So now to finish the story with James (Jim), whose diary inspired me to put pen to paper recording his life at Welbeck.

After leaving Welbeck to take up the post with Sir Dennis Bailey at Lenton, he stayed for six or seven years.

He and Edith felt they would like to become independent; they made the decision and bought their own house a few miles away from Lenton. James would become a freelance gardener. They could only hope they may be successful in their venture. He was very successful and became much sought after. The gardens he now tended were much smaller; James found it very satisfying to organise, plan and care for them. He must often have thought of Welbeck and how different his life was now after the formality he had been used to. He was also kept busy on many evenings making wreaths and bouquets.

Edith was happily settling into family life in their newly built home. A daughter, Florence May, was born, named for

47

James's sister who had died so young and of whom James had poignant memories. Later a son, Geoffrey James, arrived. It was decided not to give him James as his first name so as to avoid the confusion there had been with James and his father!

As they became established, they bought a motorbike and sidecar, quite unusual in the days before the war.

They were often making the journey to Welbeck to see the remaining family and friends.

In years to come, when war was declared in 1939, Florence joined the WAAF and was only at home during her short leaves. When she left the service, she married a fellow serviceman so never lived at home again.

When Geoffrey was called up to do his National Service in 1946, James and Edith found themselves as Darby and Joan, on their own for the first time.

However, James carried on gardening until his mid-seventies, when Edith was taken ill. She died in 1963. James was on his own until he died in 1967. It had been a long and happy marriage.

I married Geoffrey; when our first son was born, we named him James, so that the name would carry on although we actually used the derivative of Jim.

Although Harry had three sons, none carried their grandfather's name. With Edgar's death and Annie and Ernest unable to have children, my father-in-law James was the only other brother to have a son. He and Edith named him Geoffrey but gave him James as his second name. When Geoffrey and I had our first son, we named him James for his grandfather. We had a second son whom we named Garry after one of the children listed in the Bible.

This caused confusion and some misunderstanding! Not having carefully gone through the names with father-in-law at that stage we discovered we had made somewhat of a mistake. The name, in copperplate handwriting in the Bible, certainly looked like Garry. We had to smile when we eventually discovered it was Sarry – the name by which Sarah was always known to the family. I am not sure if we are forgiven!

Sadly, Geoffrey died before either of our sons had children. I have lovely granddaughters but no grandsons.

And so, our James is the last one in this family line to carry the name.

Entrance to Welbeck Abbey

Lion Gates Welbeck

Entrance Hall Welbeck

South Lodge

Tunnel Entrance South Lodge – With Charlotte and daughters having opened the gate for the postman in the Pony and Trap

The 6th Duke of Portland

The Duchess of Portland with the Rufford Hounds

A gardener tending plants in the Palm House

James and colleague in the Palm House.

The new larger boiler arriving for installation to serve the Glasshouses.
Note: How even at work the men are wearing suits and ties

The underground Ballroom

First note from the Duchess

WELBECK ABBEY

WELBECK ABBEY,
WORKSOP, NOTTS.

Dec 14th 1911

Pagson

The Dinner table was *beautiful* last night –

The most artistic colouring & arrangement I ever saw, & I know what a long time

it must have taken time & what labour & thought!

I hope your little sister is no worse

Yours faithfully,
Portland.

Second note from the Duchess

The Library

Family Portrait 1911
L to R
Back row: Sarah, Ernest, Florence, James, Gertrude, Edgar
Front row: Polly, James Snr, Charlotte, Harry

Silver wedding 1914

Jan 1st 1916

Welbeck Abbey,
Worksop,
Notts.

Payson.

My dinner table was lovely last night — I did admire it so — *Leopold dear* the *Rosemary* — I love *Rosemary*, & send you a piece as a remembrance of the

Third note from the Duchess

pretty table! Yours truly, W Portland

Ernest tending the herbaceous borders
A former Head Gardner at Clumber Park (a nearby estate in
the Dukeries) informed me these borders were only in
existence for a short time as when the war was declared in
1914 they were cleared for vegetable growing.

The Print Corridor, Welbeck Abbey

Epilogue

Poignantly, Edwina's son James (Jim) passed away while this book was in production.

Bibliography

A history of St. Winifred's Church by his Grace the Duke of
    Portland, Edited by the Rev. Hugh McCalman M.C.
    (March 1937).

Tunnel Vision: The Enigmatic Fifth Duke of Portland by
    Derek Adlam (2003).